Prayers *for* Joy *and* Thanksgiving

David Adam
Rupert Bristow
Nick Fawcett
Susan Sayers
Ray Simpson

kevin
mayhew

Prayers compiled from:

1000 Prayers for Public Worship – David Adam
Prayers for Inclusion and Diversity – Rupert Bristow
2000 Prayers for Public Worship – Nick Fawcett
Selected Prayers for Public Worship – Nick Fawcett
More Short Prayers for Public Worship – Nick Fawcett
Prayers for All Seasons – Nick Fawcett
Prayers for All Seasons 2 – Nick Fawcett
1500 Prayers for Public Worship – Susan Sayers
His Complete Celtic Prayers – Ray Simpson

kevin mayhew

First published in Great Britain in 2013 by Kevin Mayhew Ltd
Buxhall, Stowmarket, Suffolk IP14 3BW
Tel: +44 (0) 1449 737978 Fax: +44 (0) 1449 737834
E-mail: info@kevinmayhewltd.com

www.kevinmayhew.com

ISBN 978 1 84867 594 0
Catalogue No. 1501393

Cover design by Rob Mortonson
© Images used under licence from Shutterstock Inc.
Typeset by Richard Weaver

Printed and bound in Great Britain

About the authors

DAVID ADAM was the Vicar of Lindisfarne, off the Northumbrian coast, for thirteen years until he retired in March 2003. His work involved ministering to thousands of pilgrims and other visitors. He is the author of many inspiring books on spirituality and prayer, and his Celtic writings have rekindled a keen interest in our Christian heritage.

RUPERT BRISTOW was Director of Education for Canterbury Diocese and a governor of Canterbury Christ Church University from 1995 until his retirement in 2008 and is active as a Reader in Trinity Benefice, Folkestone. He has worked in education – in schools, universities and administration – at home and overseas. He has also been a specialist adviser to a House of Commons select committee, edited and written for various educational publications and chaired Kent SACRE (Standing Advisory Council for Religious Education). He is an Honorary Fellow of Canterbury Christ Church University.

NICK FAWCETT was brought up in Southend-on-Sea, Essex, and trained for the Baptist ministry at Bristol and Oxford, before serving churches in Lancashire and Cheltenham. He subsequently spent three years as a chaplain with the Christian movement Toc H, before focusing on writing and editing, which he continues with today, despite wrestling with cancer. He lives with his wife, Deborah, and two children – Samuel and Kate – in Wellington, Somerset, worshipping at the local Anglican church. A keen walker, he delights in the beauty of the Somerset and Devon countryside around his home, his numerous books owing much to the inspiration he unfailingly finds there.

SUSAN SAYERS is the author of many popular resource books for the church. Through the conferences and workshops she is invited to lead, she has been privileged to share in the worship of many different traditions and cultures. A teacher by profession, she was ordained a priest in the Anglican Church and, before her retirement, her work was divided between the parish of Westcliff-on-Sea, the local women's prison, writing, training days and retreats.

RAY SIMPSON is a Celtic new monastic for tomorrow's world, a lecturer, consultant, liturgist, and author of some 30 books. He is the founding guardian of the international Community of Aidan and Hilda and the pioneer of its e-studies programmes. He is an ordained member of the Christian church and lives on the Holy Island of Lindisfarne. His website is www.raysimpson.org

1 Blessed are you, Lord our God,
for out of your love
you call us to know and to love you.
Lord, may we come to know you,
and in knowing you, love you,
and in loving you, serve you,
whose service is perfect freedom.
Blessed are you, Father, Son and Holy Spirit. *David Adam*

2 Blessed are you, Lord our God,
for you have called us
to know you and to love you.
You invite us to experience the joy
of coming into your presence
and to delight in your grace.
Lord, we come
depending on your grace and goodness.
Blessed are you, Father, Son and Holy Spirit.

David Adam

3 Blessed are you, Lord our God,
for you love us with an everlasting love.
We rejoice that nothing can separate us
from your love in Christ Jesus.
Lord, help us to show your love to each other at all times.
Blessed are you, Father, Son and Holy Spirit.

David Adam

4 Blessed are you, Lord our God,
for you come to us and abide with us always.
Your light scatters the darkness from before us
and you invite us to let this light shine through us
and reveal you to the world.
In your love help us to be children of light.
Blessed are you, Father, Son and Holy Spirit.

David Adam

5 Blessed are you, Lord God of all creation,
from the rising of the sun to its setting,
your glory is proclaimed in all the world.
Your presence has brought light to our darkness
and a new radiance to the world.
As you call us into this marvellous light,
may we offer our lives and talents to you,
may our lips proclaim your praise,
and may we go on our way rejoicing.
Blessed be God for ever. *David Adam*

6 Blessed are you, Lord our God,
for you have called us to seek you,
to know and to love you.
You have revealed yourself in Jesus Christ,
our Saviour and our God.
We come to worship you.
Blessed are you, Father, Son and Holy Spirit. *David Adam*

7 We give thanks for our homes and loved ones.
Through our families teach us to be sensitive
to the needs of others;
help us to listen carefully and to respond quickly.
We ask your blessing upon all
who have stopped communicating properly
with each other,
that they may again be awakened
to those with whom they live and work. *David Adam*

8 Come, Lord, let your presence be known
in our homes and in our lives.
Bless us in all our relationships
and dealings with others.
Come, Lord, with your light and love
to lives that are struggling with poverty and debt,
with bad housing and broken-down communities.

David Adam

9 We thank you for our homes
and the love and acceptance that is there.
We pray for homes where life is oppressive
or adventure smothered.
We remember all who are leaving home for the first time
and all their loved ones.
We give you thanks for homes
where there are new members of the family
and where all are growing in love. *David Adam*

10 Blessed are you, Lord God.
To you be all praise and glory for ever and ever,
for you are our light and our salvation.
You created light out of darkness
and have brought your light to our lives
through the birth of your Son, our Lord Jesus Christ.
Blessed are you, Father, Son and Holy Spirit,
one God for ever and ever. *David Adam*

11 Jesus Christ, Light of the World,
scatter the darkness from about us and within us
and help us to walk as children of the light.
Help us to know that you love us
and are with us always. *David Adam*

12 Blessed are you Lord our God, Creator of light and life.
We rejoice in your presence
and seek to live fully in your light. *David Adam*

13 Blessed are you, Lord God,
for you have called us out of darkness
into your glorious light.
You seek out and save all who are lost
and willing to turn to you.
You are our God and Saviour. *David Adam*

14 Blessed are you, Lord our God,
for you have called us out of darkness
into your most glorious light.
In calling us, you give our lives direction and purpose:
you offer us the opportunity
to reveal your love and your presence to the world.
Blessed are you, Father, Son and Holy Spirit,
one God now and for ever. *David Adam*

15 Blessed are you, Lord our God,
for you have created light to dispel the darkness
and have shone in our hearts
to give the light of the knowledge of the glory of God
in the face of Jesus Christ.
We rejoice that all power and might come from you.
David Adam

16 By the light that destroys darkness,
bring hope and comfort to all who suffer.
We remember all whose lives are darkened
by fear or their past. *David Adam*

17 Good and gracious God,
you have rescued us from the darkness of death
and opened for us the way to eternal life.
We bring before you all our friends and loved ones
who are now with you in your kingdom.
Lord, grant them your love and light. *David Adam*

18 Let Jesus bring light to your lives.
The Lord Jesus give light to your eyes,
give light to your mind,
give light to your heart,
give light to your hands,
give light to your whole life
today and for ever. *David Adam*

19 For your love revealed in seeking us,
for your love revealed in meeting us,
for your love revealed in accepting us,
we give you thanks and praise. *David Adam*

20 Lord God, we give thanks
for your love that will not let us go.
Even when we ignore you, you still love us.
We may forget you, but you never forget us.
You seek us until the day we turn to you
and then you hold us in your love.
We give thanks that you have sought us
in Jesus Christ the Good Shepherd. *David Adam*

21 God, you created us for love and by your love.
For your love in caring for us,
for your love in providing for us,
we give you thanks and praise. *David Adam*

22 God, you love us with an everlasting love.
Nothing in all of creation
can separate us from your love.
Even when we forget you,
you do not forget or cease to love us.
In you is our hope and our strength,
through Jesus Christ our Lord. *David Adam*

23 Blessed are you, Lord our God,
for you have created us out of your love
and for your love.
You have revealed your love in Jesus Christ
and by the sending of the Spirit.
Lord, as you love us,
we give our love to you. *David Adam*

24 Lord Jesus, let your peace fill my heart,
my actions and my days.
Let your peace be known in my life,
in my work and in all my dealings.
Help me to be an instrument of your peace
and to share your peace with others. *David Adam*

25 Lord, in the stillness, speak to us;
in the emptiness, come to us and fill us;
to our troubles, come with your peace;
to our weakness, come with your strength;
in our doubts and our fears, abide with us.
Still the storms within us and let us find rest in you.
Help us to be the people you want us to be,
and to achieve what you want us to do,
that we may go out in confidence
and serve you all our days.
Through Jesus Christ our Lord, who is alive and reigns
with you and the Holy Spirit, one God now and for ever.
David Adam

26 Lord, we come to you
for peace of mind and spirit.
Teach us to rest in you and in your love
and to work for the coming of your kingdom. *David Adam*

27 Lord, you know that our lives are lived
in the midst of so many dangers:
there are storms and events
that can so easily overwhelm us.
Help us at all times to know your presence,
to be aware of your power
and to rest in your peace. *David Adam*

28 Blessed are you, Lord God, Creator of all life.
We thank you because we are wonderfully made.
You have given us the gift of communication:
eyes to see, ears to hear and lips to speak.
Teach us not only to speak to you but to listen,
to be quiet in your presence
and know that you are God. *David Adam*

29 God, you are always with us;
you never leave us.
Help us to come before you in quietness and stillness,
that we may know your power and your peace. *David Adam*

30 Praise and glory to you, Lord God,
for you have made us.
You are our Creator and Redeemer;
you are our Guide and our Strength.
To you be glory, Father, Son and Holy Spirit. *David Adam*

31 Blessed are you, Lord, God of all creation.
The whole universe belongs to you
and yet you care for each one of us.
You come to us in love to be our Saviour and our friend.
You have chosen us to be your people
and given us of your Holy Spirit.
We give you thanks and praise. *David Adam*

32 Gracious God, we give you thanks and praise
for our fellowship and friendship,
for our talents and our sharing,
for our growth and our learning,
for our faith and our hope,
for the firm foundation of Christ. *David Adam*

33 Blessed are you, Lord God,
Giver of life and Creator of love.
We give you thanks and praise
for the light of each day
and for the light of the Gospel
as revealed in our Saviour Jesus Christ.
We rejoice in the life that you give us
and we delight in your presence. *David Adam*

34 We give thanks for all who have shown us
love and forgiveness,
for those who loved us
even when we hurt them by our actions.
We pray for all who love us and share our lives.
David Adam

35 Blessed are you, Father, Son and Holy Spirit,
the one and only God:
to you be praise and glory for ever.
We love you, O God, with all our heart, with all our soul,
with all our mind and with all our strength.
We come to give ourselves to you
as you give yourself to us.
Blessed be God for ever. *David Adam*

36 God, we give thanks to you
for your love towards all peoples of the world.
You have chosen to give yourself to us all
and invite us to give ourselves to you.
Blessed are you, Lord God, for all things come from you
and of your own do we give you.
We come in our poverty to your riches,
in our foolishness to your wisdom,
in our sorrows to your healing and joy. *David Adam*

37 The love of the Father enfold you.
The love of the Saviour uphold you.
The love of the Spirit surround you.
May you find in God a sure foundation:
and the blessing of the Almighty
be upon you now and for ever. *David Adam*

38 Heavenly Father,
as we thank you for your gifts,
let us love you with our hearts.
As we love you in our hearts,
let us know you in our soul.
Give us strength to so take you into our lives
that we show you in our approach to others.
Give us the desire to so show you in our actions
that we transmit your love and extend your kingdom.

Rupert Bristow

39 Father, Son and Holy Spirit,
you are indivisible yet stand alone.
Make us appreciate the importance
of solitude and community
in our lives and in our hearts.
We ask this through the love of the one who sets us free
yet brings us home,
your Son, our Saviour,
Jesus Christ.

Rupert Bristow

40 Father of all,
we owe you everything in life,
our hopes, our dreams, our loves.
May we always respect those who choose solitude,
as the desert fathers did and as hermits still do.
But may we be tolerant of those who need others,
to talk to, to complain to, to listen to, to command or obey.
May we have the right balance in our lives,
in families as well as friendships.

Rupert Bristow

41 God of mercy,
we thank you for the unifying force of prayer,
across borders, across generations.
Make prayer our delight and our guide,
when together, when apart,
in good times and bad.
May the light of the world
be a beacon for creative solitude
as well as community cohesion,
throughout our lives.

Rupert Bristow

42 God of life,
bless our human habitations,
in city and country, town or village.
Look down with favour on our land
and the places where all your people live.
We thank you for the sheer variety
in our landscape, in our city streets,
in the cultures and languages across the world.

Rupert Bristow

43 Lord of land and sea,
let our hearts leap and our spirits soar
as we behold a rainbow in the sky.
And may the beauty of sunset
be as glorious over our seas and hills,
as over our cityscapes and beautiful bridges.
May our built environment echo the natural world,
so that we can be proud of both.
And wherever we live,
may we appreciate and protect our environment.

Rupert Bristow

44 Heavenly Father,
thank you for the countryside,
for the flowers, trees and crops
as well as the rolling hills and winding streams.
Whether we live in town or country,
help us to appreciate the variety of our world.
Bring us a glimpse of heaven
in hedgerow and copse,
a scent of eternity
in honeysuckle and lavender. *Rupert Bristow*

45 Lord of lords,
we are your unworthy servants,
but make us worthy of your love,
not only in our prayers and praise,
but in our lives,
the way we love,
the way we trust,
the way we work,
the way we are,
the way we thank you,
through Jesus Christ, our Lord. *Rupert Bristow*

46 Lord of truth and beauty,
we know that you have created all things,
seen and unseen, known and unknown.
We give thanks for all that is beautiful,
but also everything that is useful.

Where both go hand in hand, thank you.
Where we find the one or the other,
we nevertheless praise your handiwork, Lord.

Rupert Bristow

47 God of great gifts,
let us rejoice in the great purpose you have for us,
and also the means you have given us
to carry out your mission.
Let us always be aware of the greatest story ever told,
in how we lead our lives.
The beauty of Bethlehem
was not in finery or show,
but in generosity, humility, purpose and love.
Let us remember – and be glad. *Rupert Bristow*

48 Lord of mind and spirit,
give us a true appreciation of celestial sounds,
in music, in voice, in words, in prayer.
May the gift of silence crowd out the sound of noise.
May we value balance in all things,
rhythm in most things,
and harmony as well as melody. *Rupert Bristow*

49 God of vision and purpose,
give us the goal of meeting our potential,
in a world where you have shown
that nothing is impossible with you.
Put us to work to your greater glory.
And along the way may we appreciate
the joys of excellence
in those who have practised and sharpened their skills,
spiritually and physically, to your glory. *Rupert Bristow*

50 Sovereign God,
for the rich promise of each day,
so full of possibilities, so awash with potential,
and for the still greater anticipation of the life to come
stretching out into eternity,
we lift up our hearts in grateful worship and
heartfelt praise. *Nick Fawcett*

51 Living God,
for the joy of life, the joy of faith,
the joy of knowing you,
we give you our grateful praise. *Nick Fawcett*

52 Sovereign God,
we can hardly begin to comprehend your power,
barely grasp the extent of your love
and scarcely start to fathom the awesome breadth of your purpose:
we glimpse only a little of the truth,
yet that little causes us to gasp in wonder and kneel in homage.
Receive our praise,
for we offer it in humble and reverent worship,
through Jesus Christ our Lord. *Nick Fawcett*

53 Lord Jesus Christ,
meet with us afresh each day,
and open our eyes to see you,
our ears to hear you,
our minds to know you
and our hearts to love you.
So may we glimpse a little more of your glory
and our lives sing your praises in joyful worship.
Nick Fawcett

54 Sovereign God,
your greatness fills the heavens,
your power sustains the universe,
your love supports all creation
and your purpose extends to all times
and all people,
yet you have time for the very least of us –
time for all!
For that most awesome of truths,
we give you our praise. *Nick Fawcett*

55 Almighty God,
yours is the hand that created the universe,
the power that shapes the course of history,
the love that moves through all things
and the grace that opens up the way to life,
yet all that is merely a fraction of your greatness.
Receive our praise,
and open our hearts to know you better each day,
until that great day when we meet you face to face
and rejoice in the wonder of your presence,
through the grace of Christ. *Nick Fawcett*

56 Living God,
remind us that,
though you are far above all human thought,
you are always near,
made known through Christ
and dwelling within us through your Holy Spirit.
Receive our grateful praise. *Nick Fawcett*

57 Mighty God,
though we stretch imagination to the limit,
we barely begin to glimpse how wonderful you are.
Though you sometimes seem distant,
you are ever near.
Whatever we face,
wherever we are,
you are there,
seen or unseen,
your hand always at work.
For the constancy of your love
and the faithfulness of your purpose,
we give you our praise,
in the name of Christ. *Nick Fawcett*

58 Sovereign God,
we cannot praise you too much.
Forgive us that we fail to praise you enough. *Nick Fawcett*

59 Almighty God,
open our eyes afresh to your greatness,
your power and your sovereignty over all.
Give us again a glimpse of your glory,
not just here but everywhere,
not just today but every day,
so that our hearts may be overwhelmed by your splendour
and our souls may soar in exultation
and in joyful, reverent praise. *Nick Fawcett*

60 Living God,
for your greatness beyond imagining,
your grace beyond deserving,
your goodness beyond measuring
and your love beyond comparing,
we give you our praise in awe and wonder. *Nick Fawcett*

61 Living God,
you have given us joy that knows no bounds,
mercy beyond all our deserving,
hope that can never be exhausted,
peace that passes understanding
and love that exceeds anything we can ever ask or think of.
To you be glory, praise and honour,
now and always. *Nick Fawcett*

62 To you, O God,
be praise and glory,
worship and adoration,
today and always. *Nick Fawcett*

63 Gracious God,
you bless us beyond our imagining,
love us beyond our dreaming,
forgive us beyond our deserving
and use us beyond our hoping.
To you be praise and thanksgiving,
honour and adoration,
now and always. *Nick Fawcett*

64 Living God,
for your love beyond price
and your goodness beyond measure,
receive our praise,
in the name of Christ. *Nick Fawcett*

65 Lord Jesus Christ, our Saviour,
able to keep our foot from slipping
and to present us faultless and brimming over with joy
into the glorious presence of God,
to you be glory and majesty,
dominion and power,
now and for evermore.

Adapted from Jude 24 *Nick Fawcett*

66 Sovereign God,
for opening through Christ the way to know and love you,
receive our praise. *Nick Fawcett*

67 God of life,
we acclaim you.
God of grace,
we salute you.
God of power,
we extol you.
God of love,
we praise you.
Receive the worship and devotion we offer,
for we bring them in joyful response and heartfelt worship.

Nick Fawcett

68 Great and wonderful God,
words fail us in your presence,
yet we cannot keep silent;
our minds reel in awe and wonder,
yet we yearn to know you more;
your ways are not our ways,
nor your thoughts our thoughts,
but our hearts are restless within us
and our spirits troubled
until we find our home in you.

Draw near, then, as we worship,
and, by your grace, enlarge our understanding,
enrich our faith,
and enfold us in your love,
so that knowing you more fully,
we may serve you more truly,
through Jesus Christ our Lord. *Nick Fawcett*

69 Lord Jesus Christ,
however much we think we know you,
however clearly we believe we have understood your greatness,
open our eyes today to a deeper awareness,
fuller picture
and yet more wonderful vision of who and what you are.
Teach us that our minds can only begin to grasp your glory,
at best glimpsing part of the truth,
for there is always more to be revealed,
more to learn,
more to catch our imagination and thrill our souls.
Grant, then, as we worship you,
that your radiance might burst afresh into our lives,
so that we might return to the daily routine
determined to know, love and serve you better,
to the glory of your name. *Nick Fawcett*

70 Lord Jesus Christ,
as we come to worship, give us a sense of awe and wonder,
an awareness of the privilege we have in knowing you,
receiving your Spirit
and being called your people.
Grant us a glimpse of your glory that brings home to us
your greatness and goodness,
care and compassion,
purpose and pardon –
a foretaste that fills us with joy
and causes us to kneel in adoration,
overcome with amazement, thankfulness and love.
Teach us never to become casual in our devotion,

blasé, complacent or indifferent,
but to come rather with reverence and humility,
eager to offer you, through word and deed,
the adulation you deserve.
In your name we pray. *Nick Fawcett*

71 Almighty and everlasting God,
with awe and wonder we come to worship you.
You are higher than our highest thoughts
but always close by our side;
greater than we can ever imagine
yet made known to us in Christ;
all powerful
but nurturing us as a mother tends her child;
constantly at work in human history
yet having a special concern for every one of us.
Though we stretch imagination to the limit
we barely begin to glimpse how wonderful you are.
Though you sometimes seem distant,
always you are near.
Almighty and everlasting God,
give us humility to acknowledge our weakness beside
your greatness,
faith to trust in you despite our doubts,
joy in knowing you despite the limitations of our
understanding,
and peace in serving you,
knowing that you are the Lord of all,
a God both near and far.
In Christ's name we ask it. *Nick Fawcett*

72 Almighty God,
we will never grasp the whole truth about you,
nor even a fraction of it,
but what we do see, when we take time to look,
is enough still to fill us with awe and wonder.
You are the Lord of all,
the Creator of the ends of the earth,
the giver and sustainer of life.

You are all good,
all loving,
all merciful,
involved in every moment of every day.
Forgive us that we sometimes take that for granted,
our hearts no longer thrilling as they once did
to the majesty of your presence.
Forgive us for growing so accustomed to you
that we become careless in our relationship,
losing our sense of reverence as we come to worship you.
Open our eyes afresh to your greatness,
your power,
your sovereignty over all.
Give us again a glimpse of your glory,
through Jesus Christ our Lord. *Nick Fawcett*

73 Almighty and most wonderful God,
unsearchable and inexhaustible,
greater than we can ever imagine,
higher than our highest thoughts,
enthroned in glory and splendour,
we offer again our worship,
recognising that your ways are not our ways,
nor your thoughts our thoughts.
Forgive us for forgetting that truth,
imagining that we know all there is to know about you.
Forgive us our narrow vision and closed minds,
the way we have tied you down to our own understanding,
closing our hearts to anything that challenges our
restricted horizons,
and so losing sight of your greatness.
Remind us that you have always more to say,
more to reveal and more to do.
Open our eyes, minds and hearts to who and what you are,
and so fill us with awe and wonder,
joy and thanksgiving,
praise and worship,
now and for evermore. *Nick Fawcett*

74 Great and wonderful God,
you have blessed us in so much,
showering us with your love and blessings.
Your goodness is greater than we can ever hope to measure,
your love beyond anything we can even begin to fathom,
your gifts more than we can start to number,
and yet we know you as a living reality in our hearts,
as the one who gives shape and purpose to all of life.
So we come to you with grateful hearts in joyful homage,
seeking, as best we can, to make our response.
We consecrate this time to pray,
to read,
to think
and to learn.
We acknowledge you as our Creator,
our Lord,
our Father
and our friend,
and we thank you for your incredible and unfailing love.
Accept now our worship,
poor though it is and inadequate though our words may be,
for we bring it to you as an expression of our gratitude
and a sign of our commitment,
through Jesus Christ our Lord. *Nick Fawcett*

75 Mighty God,
enthroned in splendour,
crowned with glory,
ruler over all,
we owe our life to you.
Eternal God,
moving throughout history,
giving your word,
calling your people,
we owe our hope to you.
Living God,
full of love,
full of kindness,
full of compassion,
we owe our joy to you.

Gentle God,
speaking through your Spirit,
through the quietness,
through your still, small voice,
we owe our peace to you.
Gracious God,
abounding in love,
slow to anger,
rich in mercy,
we owe our all to you.
Lord of all,
our strength and shield,
our rock and our fortress,
our God and our Redeemer,
we owe our worship to you.
Receive our praise,
through Jesus Christ our Lord. *Nick Fawcett*

76 Loving God,
we bring you our worship not because we must but because we may,
not because we have to but because we want to.
We come not out of duty but as a privilege,
not because it is expected of us
but because you have graciously invited us to respond.
Receive our joyful worship and glad thanksgiving,
our love, our faith and our service,
for we offer them freely to you
just as you offered yourself freely for us,
through our Lord and Saviour,
Jesus Christ. *Nick Fawcett*

77 Loving God,
we praise you that you do not just give us happiness,
but also joy;
a sense of celebration that bubbles up within us,
irrepressible and indestructible.
We thank you that even when life is hard,
even when we are confronted by tragedy and disaster,
there is always a reason to rejoice,

springing from a confidence in your eternal purpose.
Help us to open our lives more fully to you each day,
so that our joy may be complete
and may communicate itself to others in such a way
that they too may come to celebrate your love
and exult in your blessing,
through Jesus Christ our Lord. *Nick Fawcett*

78 Sovereign God,
we thank you that you came in Christ
not to exact punishment but to show mercy;
not to restrict but to liberate;
not to deny but to affirm.
Forgive us for sometimes turning joyful faith into sombre religion,
the living gospel into lifeless dogma,
a message of hope into a foretelling of doom.
Teach us to receive the gifts you want us to enjoy
and to turn life into a celebration of your goodness.
So may the people we are,
as well as the words we say,
truly proclaim the good news of Jesus Christ.
In his name we ask it. *Nick Fawcett*

79 Gracious Lord,
be a blessing to us,
leading us in the way of peace,
wisdom, love and humility,
so that we, in turn,
may be a blessing to others,
to the glory of your name. *Nick Fawcett*

80 Lord Jesus Christ,
nourish us through your word,
nurture us through your grace,
feed us through your Spirit,
fill us with your love,
for your name's sake. *Nick Fawcett*

81 Thank you, Lord,
that in pleasure and pain,
triumph and tragedy,
hope and fear,
health and sickness,
you've been with us across another year,
leading us safely through its ups and downs,
highs and lows.
Teach us,
recalling your faithful guidance,
to trust you for all that lies ahead,
knowing that you alone will be the same,
yesterday, today and tomorrow. *Nick Fawcett*

82 Living God,
as we come together on this last day of the year,
we thank and praise you
for the way you have led us through good and bad,
joy and sorrow,
hope and disappointment,
pleasure and pain.
We thank you for the way you have led us as individuals –
the experiences we have gone through,
challenges we have faced,
and victories achieved;
the people we have met,
places we have visited,
and sights we have seen;
the inspiration you have offered,
guidance provided,
and strength given.
We thank you for the way you have led us as a church –
the things learned,
fun enjoyed,
and friendship shared;
the worship offered,
faith nurtured,
and service given;

the plans made,
ventures attempted,
and successes achieved.
We praise you that we can come now in confidence,
knowing from experience
that you will be with us in the days ahead,
looking to lead us forward into new experiences of your love,
and seeking to help us grow in grace,
your power sufficient for all our needs,
whatever we may face.
Receive, then, the worship we bring,
the service we offer
and the people we are,
as individuals and as a church together.
We commit all to you,
rejoicing in your goodness,
sure of your grace,
and trusting in your eternal purpose.
Through Jesus Christ our Lord. *Nick Fawcett*

83 Lord of all,
may joy bubble up within us like a living spring,
a bubbling brook,
a gushing stream,
a mighty river,
flowing out to all we meet
and carrying them along on the tide of your love,
in jubilant celebration,
through Jesus Christ our Lord. *Nick Fawcett*

84 Loving God,
you have given us news of great joy –
teach us to celebrate that truth each day. *Nick Fawcett*

85 Gracious God,
you have given us good news for all the world,
glad tidings beyond imagining:
forgive us that so often we fail to reflect that in our lives.

Teach us to live each day in a spirit of spontaneous rejoicing
that testifies,
in a way words can scarcely begin to express,
to the matchless love and awesome gift of Christ our Lord.
Nick Fawcett

86 Living God,
you gave yourself wholly to us in Christ,
glad to call us your children.
Teach us to give ourselves similarly to you,
proud to call you our Father
and happy to be identified with your Son.
In his name we ask it. *Nick Fawcett*

87 Gracious God,
teach us to celebrate the innumerable blessings
you shower upon us each day,
and teach us also to recognise that this world
offers only a foretaste of the riches you hold in store.
Teach us to celebrate all we have received,
but to set our hearts first on your kingdom
and to show our gratitude for all your many gifts
by offering back our lives in your service,
to the glory of your name. *Nick Fawcett*

88 Loving Lord,
we have celebrated the wonder of your grace,
the breadth of your goodness
and the awesome greatness of your purpose:
so now we go on our way,
our hearts singing within us,
knowing that, as you have blessed us,
so you will continue to shower us with your love,
this and every day.
Receive our praise. *Nick Fawcett*

89 Loving God,
you gave without counting the cost,
your sole desire to share your love and
help us to give back to you,
not as a duty or an afterthought,
but as a joyful privilege,
a giving of our best,
an offering from the heart.
Take what we are and consecrate it to your service,
in the name of Christ. *Nick Fawcett*

90 Living God,
teach us to give as gladly,
as lovingly and as unreservedly to you
as you have given to us. *Nick Fawcett*

91 Gracious God,
may the joy with which you have flooded our hearts
flow freely from us,
bringing joy to others in turn,
to the glory of your name. *Nick Fawcett*

92 Living God,
teach us that your love will never let us go,
and so help us to make our response
and bring our lives to you in joyful homage,
knowing that you will continue to lead us until our
journey's end,
through Jesus Christ our Lord. *Nick Fawcett*

93 Loving God,
in all the serious business of life,
with its pathos and difficulties, trials and tragedies,
help us to see also the humorous side
and to laugh even through the tears. *Nick Fawcett*

94 Lord of all,
teach us never to laugh at others,
but, when appropriate, to laugh with them,
joyfully celebrating your gift of life in all its richness.
Nick Fawcett

Gracious Lord,
send us out with laughter in our eyes,
a smile on our lips,
a song in our heart and merriment in our soul,
and so may we share the joy that you have given us,
to the glory of your name. *Nick Fawcett*

96 Gracious God,
for your blessing beyond deserving,
your mercy beyond all reason
and your love that knows no bounds
receive our praise and help us to show our gratitude
by showing the same compassion in our dealings with others
as you have shown to us. *Nick Fawcett*

97 Gracious God,
we thank you for loving us before we ever loved you,
and for continuing to love us
even when we find it hard to love ourselves.
Teach us to accept what we are
and so to grow into what we can become. *Nick Fawcett*

98 Living God,
may your love flow to us,
reaching down to bless and within to bring joy.
May your love flow through us,
reaching upwards in worship and outwards in service.
May your love kindle our love,
to the glory of your name. *Nick Fawcett*

99 Lord Jesus Christ,
help us to look to you who showed us love in action –
a love that stays true,
trusts, hopes and perseveres in all things –
and help us truly to realise that, without such love,
all our words, faith and religion count for nothing.
Nick Fawcett

100 Lord Jesus,
we bring all we are before you –
the bad as well as the good,
the doubt as well as the faith,
the sorrow as well as the joy,
the despair as well as the hope –
knowing that you love us so much that you died for us
despite it all.
Receive our praise. *Nick Fawcett*

101 Gracious God,
so dwell within us that we will rejoice each day at all
your mercies
and love you with heart and soul and mind. *Nick Fawcett*

102 Gracious God,
take our love for you and fan it into a mighty flame
so that we may love you as you deserve,
to the glory of your name. *Nick Fawcett*

103 Lord Jesus Christ,
live in our hearts, fill our souls,
renew our minds,
so that we may know and love you fully,
just as you know and love us. *Nick Fawcett*

104 Sovereign God,
teach us what it means to love you with body, mind and soul,
and help us to be as committed to you as you are to us,
through Jesus Christ our Lord. *Nick Fawcett*

105 Lord Jesus Christ,
teach us to love as you love,
and to offer you the devotion you deserve
and that you so freely show to all. *Nick Fawcett*

106 God of all,
break through the barriers that shut our minds fast,
and help us to see things both as they really are
and as you can help them become.
Move within us,
in the name of Christ. *Nick Fawcett*

107 Gracious God,
help us to open our lives to your searching gaze
and our hearts to your redeeming love. *Nick Fawcett*

108 Gracious God,
teach us that before we can give anything,
we need first to receive,
and so open our lives to your saving, renewing love,
through Christ our Lord. *Nick Fawcett*

109 Lord Jesus Christ,
show us those areas of our lives that are closed to your love,
and help us to open them fully to you,
so that you may live in us and work through us,
to the glory of your name. *Nick Fawcett*

110 Gracious God,
give us courage, faith and humility to let go of hatred
and to follow the way of love,
through Jesus Christ our Lord. *Nick Fawcett*

111 Gracious God,
take the little love we have,
nurture, deepen, and expand it,
until we have learned what love really means,
until your love flows through our hearts,
until love is all in all. *Nick Fawcett*

112 Gracious God,
teach us the secret of a love that goes on loving,
despite all it faces. *Nick Fawcett*

113 Lord Jesus Christ,
come to us, live in us, love through us. *Nick Fawcett*

114 Lord Jesus Christ,
you know what it is to give,
for you gave your all.
Teach us that whatever we give,
we shall receive far more,
and so use us to show your love and bring your blessing to others,
to the glory of your name. *Nick Fawcett*

115 Lord Jesus Christ,
you tell us that the whole law is summed up in the command to love:
help us to understand what that means,
so that this truth may shape our decisions,
our attitudes and our life. *Nick Fawcett*

116 Gracious God,
for your gracious love that no one deserves yet all can receive,
we give you our praise.
Teach us to love in turn,
through Jesus Christ our Lord. *Nick Fawcett*

117 Living God,
we want to love you,
we want to love others,
but we're not very good at doing either.
Today, as we worship you,
teach us more of what love really means.
Speak to us through Christ,
and, through your Holy Spirit,
equip us to follow his way,
turning the other cheek,
going the extra mile,
praying for our enemies,
giving without counting the cost.
Help us to love as fully as you love us,
to your glory. *Nick Fawcett*

118 Sovereign and saving God,
for your mercy that redeems us
and your love that welcomes us
we praise you.
We deserve nothing
and yet you gave all to bring us life,
now and always.
Help us today to grasp the extent of your love,
the breadth of your purpose
and the scope of your grace –
to recognise that no one is beyond your mercy
or outside your concern.
Teach us, then, to be generous in our dealings with others,
as you have dealt so generously with us,
through Jesus Christ our Lord. *Nick Fawcett*

119 Living God,
help us to understand more clearly today
that loving you must show itself in loving others;
that commitment should spill over into compassion,
faith into works
and prayer into service.
Open our eyes to the needs of our neighbours,
both near and far,
and help us wherever possible
to express something of your care and concern for all,
ministering to them in the name of Christ. *Nick Fawcett*

120 Sovereign God,
remind us again today of what really matters to you,
what alone breathes life into worship and service,
all else being as nothing without it –
the gift of love.
Teach us that around this greatest of attributes
revolve the two greatest commandments –
to love you
and others –
and so, we pray, put your love within us,
so that it may underlie all we offer now
and do always.

Fill our lives to overflowing,
so that we will truly love you
with all our heart, understanding and strength,
and love our neighbour as ourselves,
through Jesus Christ our Lord. *Nick Fawcett*

121 Lord of all,
fill us with love,
so that we might truly worship you.
May all we say, think and do come from the heart,
inspired by love in return,
and offered to you not because it's expected of us
but because we yearn to express our devotion,
to show you how much you mean to us
and how thankful we are
for the difference you've made to our lives. *Nick Fawcett*

122 Sovereign God,
teach us to love without demanding we are loved first,
to serve without expecting service in return,
to show compassion to others
even when they care nothing about us.
Remind us, as we worship you,
that you have shown just such love to us in Christ,
just such service, generosity and compassion,
and, by your grace, grant that something of you
may shine through us,
to the glory of your name. *Nick Fawcett*

123 Sovereign God,
remind us through this time of worship of the essentials
of faith –
love for you and love for others –
and through our being here today
nurture such love within our lives.
Touch our hearts through your Spirit,
and renew us through the grace of Christ,
so that our devotion to you and to the good of others
may be as real as that you so faithfully show us.
Help us now truly to love you with heart and mind and soul,
and to love our neighbour as ourselves. *Nick Fawcett*

124 Sovereign God,
give us a sense of your nearness as we worship you,
so that we might hear your voice
and learn more of your love in Christ.
Teach us through his life and ministry,
and through all those who, across the years,
have experienced his power
and felt the touch of his hand in their lives,
to respond in turn,
bringing our broken lives and broken world to him,
and opening all to his healing, restoring and life-giving love.

Nick Fawcett

125 Gracious God,
for all our talk of love we rarely actually show it.
We profess devotion, so long as nothing too much is asked of us.
We show affection, provided affection is returned.
Almost always, our love is conditional,
as much about us as its intended object,
dependent on our criteria,
tied to our expectations.
Your love is so very different,
constantly flowing out despite our unworthiness,
despite everything about us that is unlovable.
You carry on reaching out though we reject you.
You continue to care for us though we care nothing for you.
Your love is qualified by no conditions,
being entirely about us rather than you,
our welfare,
our joy.
Gracious God,
you don't just talk about love –
you show it day after day,
for quite simply you are love!
To you be praise and glory,
now and for ever.

Nick Fawcett

126 Lord Jesus Christ,
before we ever loved you, you loved us;
before we ever looked for you, you were seeking us out;
before we ever made a response, you were guiding our footsteps.
Always you have been there taking the initiative,
just as you did throughout your ministry
and even at the time of your death.
In love you offered your life,
and in love you continue to reach out,
never resting until our journey is over
and the race is won.
To you be praise and glory,
honour and thanksgiving,
now and for evermore. *Nick Fawcett*

127 Gracious God,
it is wonderful enough that you bother to look for us at all;
more wonderful still that you keep on looking day after day,
year after year,
until you have found us.
No matter what we do or how often we fail,
still we matter to you,
enough for you never to rest until we are restored to your side.
Teach us to recognise the astonishing breadth of your love,
and to respond with gratitude
in faithful service
and joyful praise,
to your glory. *Nick Fawcett*

128 Gracious God,
we praise you that, above all else, you are a God of love –
not of judgement, anger or vengeance,
but of constant and total love.
Though we repeatedly fail you,
turning our back on your goodness,
still you continue to love us,
fiercely and wholeheartedly.

Though we turn away from you,
wilfully rejecting your guidance
and repeatedly betraying your trust,
still you long to take us back,
to restore a living, loving relationship with you.
For this awesome love,
greater than words can express,
deeper than we can begin to understand
and more passionate than anything else we shall ever experience,
we give you our thanks and offer our worship,
in the name of Christ. *Nick Fawcett*

129 Gracious God,
we talk often about love,
but we have little idea what it really is.
The love we show to others is invariably flawed,
corrupted by ulterior motives and self-interest.
We can scarcely begin to fathom the immensity of the love you hold for us;
a love that is inexhaustible,
awesome in its intensity,
devoted beyond measure.
Forgive us for losing sight of this one great reality at the heart of faith
without which all else is as nothing.
Forgive us for portraying you as a God of vengeance and justice
when, above all, you are a God of love,
a God who, despite our repeated disobedience,
refuses to let us go.
Teach us to open our hearts to all you so freely give us,
and so may we love you and others
with something of that same total commitment.
We ask it in the name of Christ. *Nick Fawcett*

130 Lord God,
so many words are used to describe you,
in an attempt to sum up just who and what you are.

We speak of your power, might and majesty
to express your greatness.
We label you eternal, everlasting, infinite
to convey your timelessness.
We speak of your justice, righteousness and holiness
to encapsulate your otherness.
We call you Creator, Father, Redeemer
to articulate your goodness.
Yet all these words fall short,
pointing to part but not all of the truth.
We praise you, though, that there is one word that says it all –
that little word 'love'.
However overworked the term may be,
it nonetheless sums up your whole nature, purpose and being.
So, then, may we live each day,
assured that, whatever may be,
your love will always enfold us until it finally conquers all.
Lord God,
we praise you,
through Jesus Christ our Lord. *Nick Fawcett*

131 Lord Jesus Christ,
like so many others we yield to pressures to conform
in our yearning for acceptance.
We wear a socially acceptable mask,
say the right words
and do what's expected of us rather than risk rejection,
even when it means pretending to be what we are not.
We are so used to acceptance being conditional
that we find it hard not to approach you in the same way,
feeling that we must measure up to some yardstick
of what is pleasing to you.
Teach us that your love is not like that.
Help us to recognise that even when we fail you,
your love is not withdrawn.
May the knowledge that you accept us as we are
help us each day to become more fully the person we can be,
through your saving grace. *Nick Fawcett*

132 Lord Jesus Christ,
we are reminded today that you didn't just accept death for our sake
but chose it;
that you didn't simply let things happen
but planned them in advance,
knowing the way you would take,
down to that final agony on the cross.
You staked all,
you gave all,
and you did it willingly for the sake of people like us.
Such love is too wonderful to comprehend,
but we thank you for it with all our hearts,
and offer you our joyful praise in glad response.

Nick Fawcett

133 Lord Jesus Christ,
you came to our world as light in its darkness.
You came out of love,
bringing life, hope and forgiveness.
You came not to condemn but to save,
not to judge but to show mercy.
You came willingly enduring darkness for our sakes:
the darkness of loneliness and rejection,
of betrayal and denial,
of suffering and humiliation,
of fear and death,
of all our human sinfulness carried on your shoulders.
Lord Jesus Christ,
we thank you,
we praise you,
and we worship you.

Nick Fawcett

134 Lord Jesus Christ,
you didn't just talk about love;
time and time again you showed it.
And you loved not just those who loved you,
but your enemies equally,
those who you knew were intent on destroying you
by whatever means necessary.

We stand ashamed, in contrast,
our own love so weak,
so limited,
so dependent on its object.
Even loving our friends is hard enough;
to love our enemies is beyond us;
and yet we know that only this can break the cycle
of hatred, suspicion and fear,
which so divides our world.
Lord Jesus,
we cannot achieve it ourselves,
but, we ask you, move within us,
touch our hearts,
and teach us to love,
for your name's sake. *Nick Fawcett*

135 Lord Jesus Christ,
forgive us that so often we love only ourselves,
our every thought for our own welfare,
our own ends,
our own esteem,
our own pleasures.
Forgive us that, at best, we reserve our love for the exclusive few –
family, friends and relations.
Teach us to reach out to this troubled, divided world,
recognising the call of our neighbour in the cry of the needy.
Teach us what it means to belong not just to the community of faith
but also to the family of humankind,
and in serving them may we equally serve you,
to the glory of your name. *Nick Fawcett*

136 Lord,
we are told that the strongest survive –
that in this world it's a question of never mind the rest
so long as we're all right.
Yet you call us to another way –
to the way of humility, sacrifice and self-denial.

You stand accepted wisdom on its head,
claiming that the meek shall inherit the earth
and that those who are willing to lose their lives
will truly find them.
Lord,
it is hard to believe in this way of yours,
and harder still to live by it,
for it runs contrary to everything we know about human nature,
yet we have seen for ourselves that the world's way
leads so often to hurt, sorrow and division.
Give us, then, courage to live out the foolishness of the gospel,
and so to bring closer the kingdom of Christ
here on earth.
In his name we ask it. *Nick Fawcett*

137 Lord Jesus Christ,
you summed up the law in one simple word: 'love'.
Forgive us that though we often talk about love
we rarely show it in practice.
Forgive us everything in our lives that has denied that love:
the angry words and unkind comments,
the thoughtless deeds and careless actions,
the sorrow we have brought rather than joy,
the hurt rather than healing,
the care we have failed to express,
support we have refused to offer,
and forgiveness we have been unwilling to extend.
Help us to look to you who showed love in action –
a love that bears all things,
believes all things,
hopes all things,
endures all things –
and help us truly to realise that unless we have that,
then all our words, faith and religion count for nothing.
Nick Fawcett

138 Gracious God,
we marvel that you can love people like us,
for there is so little about us that deserves it.

We look into the mirror of our souls
and we are ashamed of what we see there,
for the image is marred by greed, pride, selfishness, envy
and so much else that destroys not just others but
ourselves too.
Yet, incredibly, you value us to the point that we are
precious in your sight,
special enough even to die for.
If you can accept us, despite everything, teach us to do
the same
and, in learning to love ourselves as you do,
help us also to love others and love you,
through Jesus Christ our Lord. *Nick Fawcett*

139 Gracious God,
we do not find it easy to love ourselves,
despite the way it may seem.
We find it hard not to dwell on our weaknesses
rather than our strengths,
not to brood about mistakes and failures
rather than rejoice in the things we have achieved.
We look at ourselves
and we see the faults and ugliness
that we try to hide from the world,
and we find the reality too painful to contemplate,
so we try to push it away once more.
Gracious God,
we thank you that you love us despite all this,
that you value us not for what we might become
but for what we are.
Teach us to live each day in the light of the incredible
yet wonderful truth
that you love us completely
and want us to be at one with ourselves,
through Jesus Christ our Lord. *Nick Fawcett*

140 Creator God,
whatever the person we may have been,
help us today to glimpse the person we can be
and, by your grace, shall become,
through Jesus Christ our Lord. *Nick Fawcett*

141 God of grace,
as dawn has broken once more,
so may the light of your love dawn afresh in our hearts
and shine out of our lives,
to the glory of your name. *Nick Fawcett*

142 Loving God,
reach out to us and fill us with your peace,
so that in turn we might reach out to others,
and by your grace be a means through which you work
for harmony and reconciliation.
In the name of Christ, we ask it. *Nick Fawcett*

143 Gracious God,
when the storm rages and life is in turmoil,
when the wind blows and the waves threaten to engulf us,
grant that even then our souls will be at peace,
secure in the constancy of your love. *Nick Fawcett*

144 Gracious God,
teach us to live each day in the light of the incredible
yet wonderful truth that you love us completely
and want us to be at peace with ourselves and with you.
In Christ's name we ask it. *Nick Fawcett*

145 Lord Jesus Christ,
speak your word and calm the troubled waters of our lives,
the turmoil of mind and restlessness of spirit,
granting the peace that you alone can give.
In your name we ask it. *Nick Fawcett*

146 Teach us, Lord,
to take stock, thoughtfully, honestly and prayerfully,
so that we may see ourselves as we really are
rather than as we imagine ourselves to be. *Nick Fawcett*

147 Gracious God,
teach us not to walk unthinkingly through life
but to reflect on all we see and experience,
and thus glimpse your hand at work. *Nick Fawcett*

148 Living God,
whatever the pressures and duties of the day,
teach us to find time for stillness,
and, in seeing you there,
may we see you always and everywhere,
through the grace of Christ. *Nick Fawcett*

149 Lord of all,
we have made time and space for quietness to hear your voice.
Go with us now into the turmoil of life,
with all its noise and confusion,
all its demands and responsibilities,
and may your peace rest with us there,
this day and for evermore. *Nick Fawcett*

150 Sovereign God,
in the rush and bustle of life,
teach us to recognise the one thing worth pursuing above all else –
your awesome love revealed in Christ. *Nick Fawcett*

151 God of the still small voice,
teach us each day to find time for moments of quietness –
time to ponder,
to pray and to meditate on your gracious love.
Breathe peace within our souls,
so that we may see the demands and responsibilities of daily life
in a fresh light,

able to meet them with rekindled faith
and calm assurance,
through Jesus Christ our Lord. *Nick Fawcett*

152 Gentle and gracious God,
calm our minds where they are troubled,
ease our bodies where they are weary,
soothe our spirits where they are in turmoil.
Teach us to find our strength in stillness and quiet
and, in the love of Christ,
to find rest for our souls. *Nick Fawcett*

153 Gracious God,
so often we deny ourselves your blessing
through failing to turn to you;
failing to respond to your love
and to receive the mercy, joy, peace and new life
you so long to bring us.
We come now, therefore,
making time and space for you,
and opening our lives to all you would pour into them.
Teach us, as we welcome you today,
to welcome you equally every day and every moment,
until you finally welcome us into your eternal kingdom,
through Jesus Christ our Lord. *Nick Fawcett*

154 Lord Jesus Christ,
remind us afresh today of your transforming power,
your ability to take something ordinary
and turn it into something special.
Take, then, our worship,
and, by your Spirit, make it into something beautiful to you,
bringing you glory and stirring again our hearts within us.
Take what we are,
and by your Spirit once more create us anew,
so that our lives will speak not of our weakness
but of your saving love and gracious power,
to the glory of your name. *Nick Fawcett*

155 God of peace,
quieten our hearts
and help us to be still in your presence.
We find this so hard to do,
for our lives are full of noise and confusion,
a host of demands and responsibilities
seeming to press in upon us from every side,
consuming our time and sapping our energy.
We run here and there,
doing this and that,
always something else to think about,
another pressing matter demanding our attention –
and then suddenly,
in the middle of it all,
we stop and realise we have forgotten you,
the one we depend on to give us strength and to calm our spirits.
God of peace,
we offer you now this little space we have made
in the frantic scramble of life.
Meet with us,
so that we may return to our daily routine with a new perspective,
an inner tranquillity,
and a resolve to make time for you regularly
so that we may use all our time more effectively
in the service of your kingdom,
through Jesus Christ our Lord. *Nick Fawcett*

156 Gracious God,
we thank you for this opportunity to worship you,
these few moments set aside to listen,
to reflect,
to respond.
Forgive us that such moments are all too few;
that we allow our time with you to be crowded out
by other demands on our time.
There is always something else that needs doing –
another letter to write,

another meal to prepare,
another job to finish,
another meeting to attend –
and so it goes on,
one thing after another calling for our attention
and forcing you to the back of the queue.
Gracious God, there is much that needs to be done,
but help us to understand that there is nothing as important
as spending time in your presence,
for without your strength, your peace and your renewing touch
we lose our perspective on everything,
depriving ourselves of the resources we most need.
Help us, then, not simply to find some place for you,
but to give you pride of place,
for only then will we experience the fullness of life
you so long to give us,
through Jesus Christ our Lord. *Nick Fawcett*

157 Lord Jesus Christ,
time and again throughout your ministry you made time to be still,
to draw away from the crowds
so that in the quietness you could reflect on your calling.
You needed those moments,
just as we need them in our turn.
So now we have made a space in our lives,
away from the daily demands,
away from the usual routine.
We are here, Lord, with time for you,
in stillness and in quietness to seek your will.
Use these moments
to refresh us,
to feed us,
to challenge and inspire us.
Fill them with your love
and so may we be filled to overflowing,
by your grace. *Nick Fawcett*

158 Loving God,
we talk of peace but all too rarely find it,
for our minds are full of a multitude of concerns,
which pull us this way and that
until we feel bewildered and confused.
We hear your still small voice bidding us to let go and rest,
but always there is another call,
another demand on our attention pressing in upon us,
and before we know it your word is drowned in the noisy bustle of life.
We cannot ignore the world or our responsibilities within it,
and we would not want to,
for there is so much you have given us that is good,
but help us always to make time for you within it,
so that even when chaos seems to reign,
your quietness may fill our souls
bringing an inner calm that nothing will ever be able to shake.
In Christ's name we pray. *Nick Fawcett*

159 Sovereign God,
we are here to worship you,
having made a space in our lives to pause and reflect.
We come to listen to your word,
and to ponder in the silence what you would say to us.
We come to hear your voice,
and in the stillness to receive your guidance.
Open our eyes to your presence,
our hearts to your love
and our minds to your will.
Direct our thoughts,
enlarge our understanding,
and shape our lives,
so that we may live and work for you,
to the glory of your name. *Nick Fawcett*

160 Gracious God,
you have promised to all who love you
a peace that passes understanding.
Forgive us that we have failed to make this our own.

We rush about,
our minds preoccupied by our problems.
We brood over situations that we cannot hope to change,
magnifying them out of all proportion.
We worry about what the future may hold
instead of focusing on the present moment
and living each day as it comes.
Teach us that you hold all things in your hands
and that, even when our worries prove justified,
you will give us strength to get through.
Whatever clouds may appear on the horizon
and whatever storms life might throw against us,
may our minds be at rest,
our spirits at peace and our hearts untroubled,
through Jesus Christ our Lord. *Nick Fawcett*

161 Living God,
in the rush and bustle of each day we all too often lose sight of you,
our minds occupied by the responsibilities,
demands and difficulties confronting us.
Instead of turning to you,
we get sucked in ever deeper,
getting these out of all perspective
and denying ourselves the strength we need to meet them.
Teach us to find time for you,
if only for a few moments,
so that we may hear your voice and discern your will.
Teach us to step back and take stock,
so that we may then step forward,
renewed in faith, strengthened in spirit,
and equipped for whatever you may ask.
In Jesus' name we ask it. *Nick Fawcett*

162 Living God,
too often we rush from one thing to the next,
preoccupied with the demands and responsibilities of each day,
and wondering where we might find the strength to see us through.

Yet instead of turning to you we struggle on as best as we can.
Teach us to create space in our lives for you,
to make a few moments every day in which we can be quiet and still,
and teach us to do that not as an afterthought but instinctively,
recognising that when we give you your proper place,
everything else will fit into place as well.
In Christ's name we ask it. *Nick Fawcett*

163 Loving God,
in all the stress and rush of life it is so easy to forget you and to lose our way.
In the press of each day,
preoccupied with our problems, pursuits,
plans and responsibilities
we allow you to be crowded out.
We strive and fret over things that cannot satisfy,
we brood over what is unimportant,
frantically suppressing that sense of emptiness deep within.
Teach us to untangle ourselves from everything that enslaves us
and to open our hearts afresh to you,
so that we might find rest and nourishment for our souls
and life in all its fullness,
through Jesus Christ our Lord. *Nick Fawcett*

164 Loving God,
we live at such a hectic pace,
our lives so busy and pressurised,
with never a moment to spare.
Yet so often we forget the one thing we really need:
time to pause and ponder,
to take stock of our lives and reflect on your goodness
so that we might understand what it is that you would say to us.
Draw near to us now in these few moments of quietness.
Teach us to be still and to know your presence,
through Jesus Christ our Lord. *Nick Fawcett*

165 Loving God,
we thank you for the wonder of your creation –
the beauty of our world,
the vastness of the universe,
and the richness of our lives.
In all you have given,
teach us to see your hand.
We praise you for all you have made
and the place you have given us within creation.
You have surrounded us with so much that is good,
and we marvel at it –
plants, animals, trees, birds,
mountains, valleys, continents, oceans,
towns, cities, nations and people:
a world of infinite beauty and wonder.
We thank you that out of chaos you brought order,
an order that we can depend upon,
explore and understand,
that shapes the very pattern of our universe,
that reflects your sovereign and guiding purpose.
Loving God,
help us to appreciate the wonder of your creation,
open to the new discoveries which research daily brings.
Save us from closing our minds
to that which challenges our convictions;
from retreating into narrow thinking,
or blind prejudice,
or some ivory tower removed from the real world.
Help us to see that as our understanding of creation grows
so we glimpse more of your greatness –
our sense of awe, wonder and astonishment
enlarged by the insights of modern science.
But help us also to recognise the limitations of
scientific study –
aware of the things it can't answer as much as the things
it can,
awake to its weaknesses as well as its strengths,
open to spiritual reality as well as empirical truth.
Loving God,
give wisdom to those involved in research

and all who must legislate upon its application,
and grant your guidance to all who strive
to improve the quality of our lives through their investigations.
Teach them and us to use creation wisely,
employing its resources for good
rather than exploiting them for evil,
and thinking not simply of ourselves
but all who will follow us. *Nick Fawcett*

166 Living God,
you tell us to sing your praises,
to make music in our hearts,
to lift up our voices in joyful adoration.
We come with gladness:
receive the worship we offer.
We bring you this service of celebration –
our hymns,
our songs,
our music –
and we offer them gladly to you,
as an expression of thanksgiving,
an outpouring of praise,
and a token of our love.
Living God,
uplift us through this time together.
May it speak to us of all you have done
and continue to do through Christ,
and so may there always be a song of praise on our lips,
and music in our hearts.
We come with gladness:
receive the worship we offer,
through Jesus Christ our Lord. *Nick Fawcett*

167 Loving God, thank you for moments to let go; to forget, if only briefly, the demands and duties of each day. Thank you for opportunities to unwind and to celebrate the sheer joy of being alive. Teach us, whatever else we do, to make time and space in our lives – for us, for others and for you.

Nick Fawcett

168 Loving God,
we come this day with a song in our hearts,
to celebrate your gift of music,
to lift up our voices in glad thanksgiving,
to make a joyful noise to you!
You have given us so much to celebrate,
so much to rejoice in.
It is good to give thanks,
right to be glad,
fitting to show our joy in music and song.
So now we bring you this service –
as an act of worship,
an expression of thanksgiving,
and an outpouring of our love.
Receive our praise,
accept our songs,
and fill our hearts with joy and thanksgiving,
as we remember the wonder of your love,
and rejoice in all you have done for us.
With all the company of heaven,
we sing your praise,
through Jesus Christ our Lord. *Nick Fawcett*

169 Gracious God,
we are here to worship you –
to lift up our voices in grateful praise,
to make music together;
a joyful noise,
a new song of thanksgiving.
We do not lift up our voices only, but also our hearts –
celebrating your great goodness,
rejoicing in your awesome love,
exulting in your unfailing grace,
focusing our thoughts upon you,
on your will,
your word,
your kingdom.
We lift up our eyes –
marvelling at the breadth of your purpose,

the wonder of your creation,
the awesomeness of your love.
We lift up our lives –
offering not just our music and song,
but everything we are,
all we say and think and do,
asking that you will take us
and consecrate us to your service,
transforming our lives through your renewing power.
Gracious God,
we are here to worship you –
to lift up our voices in grateful praise,
to make music together;
a joyful noise,
a new song of thanksgiving.
Accept what we offer for the reason that we offer it –
to give you the glory that is rightfully yours,
in heaven and on earth,
now and for evermore.
Thanks be to God,
through Jesus Christ our Lord *Nick Fawcett*

170 Lord Jesus Christ,
we can never repay all we owe you,
nor even a fraction of what we have received
from your loving hand.
There are no words or deeds great enough
to thank you for all your goodness,
but we yearn to make some kind of response,
to express our gratitude for all you have done for us.
You have poured out your blessings,
day after day,
filling our lives with good things.
You have met our needs and more than our needs,
showering us with untold riches.
Receive our worship,
receive our faith,
receive our love,
for we bring them to you
as a small but simple way of saying thank you. *Nick Fawcett*

171 Great and wonderful God,
we join with the great company of your people
on earth and in heaven,
to celebrate your majesty,
to marvel at your love and to rejoice in your goodness.
You are our God,
and we praise you.
We acknowledge you as the Lord of heaven and earth,
ruler of space and time,
Creator of all,
sovereign over life and death.
We salute you as the beginning and end of all things,
the one who is greater than we can ever begin to imagine,
higher than our highest thoughts,
beyond human expression.
We affirm you as all good,
all loving and all gracious.
We bring you now our worship,
our faith and our lives,
offering them to you in grateful adoration.
You are our God,
and we praise you,
through Jesus Christ our Lord. *Nick Fawcett*

172 Lord,
we thank you for the gift of song;
for its ability to move, challenge and inspire us,
its power to express feelings of joy and sorrow, hope and despair,
its capacity to sum up our feelings in grateful hymns of praise.
Teach us when we worship to use this gift thoughtfully,
singing to you from the heart,
and offering not just the song but ourselves with it.
Teach us to reflect on the words we sing,
so that they may speak to us of all that you have done
and speak for us of all we would do for you.
O Lord,
open our lips,
and our mouth shall declare your praise. *Nick Fawcett*

173 Almighty God, thank you for guarding us, faithfully providing shelter and protection when storms brew and waves threaten to sweep us away. Thank you for the strength of your love and certainty of your promise, the knowledge that though all else may pass away your goodness will continue, solid and secure in an ever-changing universe. Whatever we face, we will not fear, for you are with us, the same yesterday, today and for ever.

Nick Fawcett

174 Loving God, thank you for the companionship of others – the way family, friends, colleagues and acquaintances all contribute to our lives, helping to shape us as people. Thank you, above all, for the fellowship of the Church – for calling us into a community of faith, your family, in order that there too we might give and receive. Open our eyes to everything we can learn from others – the support, enrichment and understanding they can offer – and to all that we can do for them in turn. Remind us that we're called not just to individual discipleship but also to shared commitment; that if we're to serve you effectively, and help others to do the same, we need them and they need us.

Nick Fawcett

175 Lord of all, keep us ever-enthused, ever-excited, by the message of your love – what you have done and continue to do through Christ our Lord. *Nick Fawcett*

176 Eternal God, we carry a host of memories in our hearts – so much we have done, so many we have known, innumerable people, places, sights and sounds that have enriched and enthralled, fashioning the people we are today. For all we have so richly received, thank you. *Nick Fawcett*

177 Lord Jesus Christ, forgive us for taking for granted the little things of life and the health that allows us to experience them. Teach us to celebrate even the simplest of moments, however mundane they may seem. *Nick Fawcett*

178 Gracious God, we have cause to celebrate, for you have blessed us so richly, showering us each day with good things, yet we so rarely appreciate it, let alone show it. We brood instead of rejoice, complain instead of give thanks, our hearts being heavy rather than dancing within us for joy. Forgive us, and teach us to count our blessings and exult in your love. *Nick Fawcett*

179 Living God, help us to spread a little happiness, contagious joy bubbling up within us. Teach us to live with a smile in our hearts and laughter on our lips, each day celebrating your love in a way that invites others to share it in turn.

Nick Fawcett

180 Loving God, we would sing a new song to you, making music in our hearts in grateful praise and worship. We would make a joyful noise, not to draw attention to ourselves but simply to celebrate your love and to share it with others. *Nick Fawcett*

181 Generous God, thank you, for, by your grace and goodness, you have put music in our souls and a song in our hearts – a melody of praise and thanksgiving at so much that transports us with wonder and thrills us deep within. Keep that joy as fresh in us tomorrow as it is today. *Nick Fawcett*

182 Loving God, thank you that when we smile, the world smiles too; that a cheerful heart brings blessing, not just to us but to others as well. Teach us to celebrate that priceless gift, costing nothing yet yielding so much; to exult in the joy of knowing you and to pass it on in turn.

Nick Fawcett

183 Thank you, Lord, that with you not just some days are special, but all of them. You have given us new life, new beginnings, cause indeed to celebrate. *Nick Fawcett*

184 Compassionate God, though much in life is touched by pathos, teach us to keep a sense of humour, able to laugh, even through tears, and smile, even in sorrow. And though much is serious, demanding a measured response and sober judgement, help us to retain a sense of fun, aware that laughter is your gift, as valuable and special as any.

Nick Fawcett

185 We want to jump for joy, Lord, for you have blessed us with love, filled us with peace and enriched us with hope.
For your great goodness and countless gifts, thank you.

Nick Fawcett

186 Living God, we want to make music for you, to live our lives as an exuberant melody of praise offered in gratitude for all you've done and everything you mean to us. It may sometimes be out of tune, more of a joyful noise than a work of art, but receive it, we pray, together with what we are and all we long to be, for it comes from the heart, with love.

Nick Fawcett

187 God of grace and mercy, you have given cause to rejoice; forgiveness, new life and blessings beyond measure.
Help us to appreciate your goodness and truly to celebrate.

Nick Fawcett

188 Lord God, you have put a new song into our mouths, a song of joy and thanksgiving, awe and celebration. We will make music to you in our hearts – a melody of praise and worship.

Nick Fawcett

189 Creator God, not even the widest of palettes of colour can compare to the one you have used in creation, even the most comprehensive selection being magnified there a million times over: in the splendour of a sunset and magic of a rainbow, the hues of the sea and glory of the sky, the tints of autumn and tapestry of a garden, the plumage of birds and loveliness of a meadow. An immeasurable

spectrum brightens every day, causing us to catch our breath in wonder and exult in spirit. For the imprint of your hand on the canvas of life, breathtaking beyond words, receive our praise. *Nick Fawcett*

190 Creator God, thank you for a world to explore, so full of beauty and with so much to excite, intrigue, enthral and enjoy. Teach us to celebrate all you have given by living each moment to the full. *Nick Fawcett*

191 Living God, thank you for the awesome variety of creation, the breathtaking diversity of life on earth – so much to intrigue, entrance, fascinate and amaze. Teach us to appreciate both the privilege and responsibility it represents, not only rejoicing at all you have given but also respecting its innate worth and dignity and playing our part in protecting it for the future, so that others may marvel in turn. *Nick Fawcett*

192 Sovereign God, thank you for the loveliness of creation, the beauty of this wonderful world – so much around us that gives a taste of heaven here on earth. *Nick Fawcett*

193 Mighty God, thank you for the miracle of life, the wonder of a newborn child, the awesomeness of your creation. Thank you for your gift of life, the richness of this world you have given, and health and strength to enjoy it. Thank you for the new life you offer in Christ, the rebirth you make possible through him, each day, each moment: a fresh start, full of promise. Living God, receive our praise.

Nick Fawcett

194 Living God, thank you for your artistry in creation: the vibrancy of a rainbow, tints of a sunset, hues of sea, sky, woodland and meadow; the feel of trees, rocks, soil and water; the sound of birds and scent of flowers – the awesome wonder of a world awash with colour, music, flavour and fragrance. Thank you that so much you have made, so much around us, offers a taste of heaven here on earth. *Nick Fawcett*

195 Lord of all, thank you for your creation: the beauty of this world and wonder of the universe. Thank you for so much that speaks of your purpose, causing us to catch our breath in awe and wonder. For the work of your hands and all it reveals of your love, receive our praise. *Nick Fawcett*

196 Sovereign God, through the loveliness of creation, moving us to joy and wonder, open our eyes to things above, captivating beyond words. *Nick Fawcett*

197 Father God, thank you, for we were heavy laden, weighed down by daily demands and duties, and you saw our need, helping us to bear what we could not carry alone. Thank you that we can cast our cares on to you and find rest for our souls. *Nick Fawcett*

198 Thank you, Lord, that however weary we may grow, you never tire, continuing to watch over us day and night. Thank you that we can rest easy, our minds at peace, secure in the knowledge that, though we sleep, you do not.

Nick Fawcett

199 Gracious God, whether we sleep or are awake, thank you that you are always there, a constant companion, daily strength, and faithful friend. Thank you that the peace you make possible is unlike anything the world can give, bringing inner stillness, quiet assurance, rest for our souls.

Nick Fawcett

200 Loving God, by day as well as by night our spirit is all too often restless, unable to find true fulfilment or inner tranquillity. Help us to let go of our fears, and to place every part of life into your hands, so that we may know the rest you promise and find true contentment – a quietness of body, mind and soul that, day or night, cannot be shaken.

Nick Fawcett

201 Almighty God, in quiet reverence and grateful worship we kneel before you, seeking a deeper sense of your presence. In the stillness, help us to know that you are God.

Nick Fawcett

202 Gracious God,
you call us to sing a new song,
to make music in our hearts,
a 'joyful noise to the Lord'.
We come today to do just that:
to enjoy the gift of music and song,
not for its own sake alone
but as an expression of our worship,
a token of our love,
a sign of our thankfulness
and a symbol of our desire to live and work for you,
lifting up not just our voices
but also everything we are
in glad and grateful response.
Bless all we bring you now,
that it might speak for us
and to us,
in Christ's name.

Nick Fawcett

203 Father God, help us, for we're always in a hurry, rushing madly from one thing to the next. Teach us that life is not a race, a battle to beat the clock, but a gift, a journey of discovery, a foretaste of eternity. Help us, then, to live each moment as it comes, celebrating the day you have made, and remembering that time itself is in your hands.

Nick Fawcett

204 Creator God, teach us to appreciate the simple but special things of life, to make time each day, if only for a moment, to stop and stare, and to celebrate the beauty of all you have made.

Nick Fawcett

205 Lord of all, teach us, whatever else needs doing, to make time to unwind and hear your voice, to be still and glimpse your presence. Save us from being so concerned with the daily demands of life that we have no time left truly to live.

Nick Fawcett

206 Father God, teach us to take things more gently, matching our pace with yours instead of hurrying from one thing to the next. Teach us that it is better sometimes to make haste slowly than to rush headlong into a new venture and then regret it afterwards. Teach us the secret of patience – the ability to trust in your timing, recognising that the journey can be as special as the destination. *Nick Fawcett*

207 Loving God, though you promise shelter when the wind blows, a haven in times of turmoil, save us from divorcing faith from life, as though commitment involves running away from the world and the challenges it brings. May moments of retreat and quiet devotion inspire us rather to fresh service and new ventures in faith. *Nick Fawcett*

208 Living God, teach us, however busy we may be, that we need sometimes to stop and relax; that if we're to function as effectively as we would wish and stay healthy in mind, body and spirit, we need to make time not just for our daily duties, nor even just for you, but also for ourselves. Give us strength for whatever we're asked to take on, but wisdom also to know when to stop. *Nick Fawcett*

209 Creator God, thank you for green spaces – meadows, parks, gardens, countryside – everywhere that we can roam free, escaping the noise of traffic, the concrete jungle, the daily routine. Thank you for places where we can relax and reflect, in tune with nature, with ourselves and with you.

Nick Fawcett

210 Eternal God, the older we get, the more it feels as though the stopwatch is ticking and time is running out, so we rush around from one thing to the next determined to cram ever more into the unforgiving minute. Yet so easily, in our

haste, we forget to enjoy what we have, to let go of striving and simply to live. Remind us that though this mortal span may be slipping away, it is just a taste of things to come; that though the days are passing, we have no cause to fret, for with you we have all the time in the world . . . and far, far beyond! *Nick Fawcett*

211 Father God, we forget that we need to switch off sometimes if we're not to end up exhausted. Teach us to appreciate the importance of being still, of taking a breather from the demands of life, however pressing they may be. Show us the difference between doing enough and doing too much, and help us to get the balance right. *Nick Fawcett*

212 We need to relax, Lord, but there's so much still to do. Help us to let go, so that, truly refreshed, we may do it better. *Nick Fawcett*

213 God of past, present and future, when we grow impatient, fretting about being made to wait; when we race around at breakneck speed, furiously striving to cram as much as possible into every day; when we begrudge a wasted hour or unfilled minute; teach us to slow down and to take things one step at a time. Whatever we need to do, whatever we want to do, may we recognise first what we can and what we can't do, and appreciate the difference. Help us always to celebrate the given moment rather than brood over the next or the last. *Nick Fawcett*

214 Gracious God, remind us that we need to pause sometimes if we're to make sense of life, time to stop and stare being essential if we're to keep things in balance and live as you intend. In the many demands and duties we face each day, teach us to make space for stillness and quiet – space for us and for you. *Nick Fawcett*

215 Thank you, Lord, for moments to relax, to forget for a time the cares of the world, the demands and duties that cling so closely, and simply to unwind, celebrating the sheer joy of being alive. *Nick Fawcett*

216 Why, Lord, do we habitually rush through life? Why are we forever in a hurry? Grant us the gift of patience and the ability to celebrate each moment, whatever it may bring. Teach us to savour the here and now, and to let go of what might be or could have been. *Nick Fawcett*

217 Loving God,
creator of the ends of the earth,
source of all that is and has been and will be,
giver of life,
we join together to worship you.
We praise you for the wonder of our world
and for the vastness of the universe;
for all that you have made,
and for the place you have given us within your creation.
Loving God,
we join together to worship you.
We marvel at the beauty and variety of this earth –
its wonderful mixture of plants, animals, trees, birds,
mountains, valleys, streams, oceans,
and so much else besides.
Loving God,
we join together to worship you.
We thank you for everything that lifts our spirit,
that moves us to wonder,
that holds our attention,
that captures our interest.
Loving God,
we join together to worship you.
We rejoice that out of chaos you brought order –
an order we can see throughout the universe;
which we can depend upon, explore and understand;
an order that reflects your sovereign purpose
and reveals your guiding hand.
Loving God,
we join together to worship you.
Loving God,
creator of life in all its fullness,
we bring you our praise,

we offer you our worship,
we make our response,
in joyful celebration.
We join together to worship you,
in the name of Christ. *Nick Fawcett*

218 Loving God,
we thank you for the world you have given us
and all within it that speaks of you.
You have blessed us in so much,
and we are glad.
We thank you for all that is beautiful;
all that causes us to catch our breath in wonder
and points to your hand in creation.
You have blessed us in so much,
and we are glad.
We thank you for the gift of love, given and received,
speaking to us of your own great love for us.
You have blessed us in so much,
and we are glad.
We thank you for family life,
reminding us of the great family of your people
to which we belong.
You have blessed us in so much,
and we are glad.
We thank you for our food, our clothes, our homes;
all the comforts we enjoy,
and the innumerable ways you provide for us.
You have blessed us in so much,
and we are glad.
We thank you for this new morning,
for the warmth of the sun and the richness of life,
giving a foretaste of your gift of eternal life.
You have blessed us in so much,
and we are glad.
Loving God,
open our eyes to your presence around us,
to your love that surrounds us each day,
and to your hand that is always at work.

You have blessed us in so much,
and we are glad.
Speak to us through both the ordinary
and the special things of life,
that through them we may know you more fully
and serve you more truly.
You have blessed us in so much,
and we are glad.
Receive then our praise and thanksgiving,
for we offer them to you
in the name of Christ our Lord. *Nick Fawcett*

219 Loving God,
we thank you for the things in life that make us laugh,
the things that bring a smile to our faces.
We thank you for a sense of humour
helping us to see the funny side of life,
enabling us to share a joke
even when it is on ourselves.
We thank you for those with the special gift
of bringing laughter to others,
bringing a little light relief
into the seriousness of our world.
Loving God,
there is a time to weep and a time to laugh,
a place for solemnity and a place for humour.
Help us to get the balance right in our lives.
Teach us to appreciate your gift of laughter,
and to share it with those around us,
in the name of Christ. *Nick Fawcett*

220 Almighty and all-loving God,
we come together in the name of the living Christ,
to confess our faith,
to acknowledge your goodness,
to celebrate your love,
and to commit our lives afresh to your service.
Greatly you have blessed us.
Joyfully we worship you.

We praise you for this opportunity to worship you,
this time set aside week by week,
this place of fellowship where we share something of your love,
and, above all, we praise you for the assurance we have
that, as we meet together,
you are here amongst us!
Greatly you have blessed us.
Joyfully we worship you.
We praise you for your great love
that has searched us out and enriched our lives,
and for your care that constantly surrounds us,
through joy and sorrow,
hope and fear,
light and darkness.
Greatly you have blessed us.
Joyfully we worship you.
We praise you for your sovereign power,
your hand that has shaped the universe,
your purpose that directs history,
your grace that transforms lives,
and your Spirit who sustains the Church.
Greatly you have blessed us.
Joyfully we worship you.
You have made us glad in so many ways,
your love beyond anything we can deserve,
your mercy inexhaustible,
and your care for us never-failing.
Greatly you have blessed us.
Joyfully we worship you.
So now we bring you this time of worship,
not so that we might withdraw from the world,
but that we might serve it more effectively in your name;
not so that we may escape from the daily routine of our lives,
but that we may consecrate every moment
and everything to you.
Greatly you have blessed us.
Joyfully we worship you.
Almighty and all-loving God,
receive our praise,
through Jesus Christ our Lord.

Nick Fawcett

221 Great and wonderful God,
we join today
as part of the great company of your people across history
to sing of your faithfulness,
to celebrate your love,
to acknowledge your mercy,
and to marvel at your awesome power.
Receive our praise,
and accept our worship.
We rejoice in all that you are –
higher than our highest thoughts,
greater than we can ever imagine,
sovereign over all,
yet making yourself known to us in human form,
sharing our humanity,
and offering us your life.
Receive our praise,
and accept our worship.
We rejoice in the awesomeness of your love –
in the fact that, even though we fail you,
even though we make time for you only in moments of need,
even though we use you for our own ends,
still you have time for us,
seeking us out, day after day.
Receive our praise,
and accept our worship.
We rejoice that you care for us as individuals –
each chosen, valued and special in your sight,
and we thank you that, as you have watched over us
during this past week,
so you are with us now and will be always,
whatever the future may hold.
Receive our praise,
and accept our worship.
We rejoice in the wonder of life,
and we thank you for health and faculties to appreciate it,
food and clothing to sustain it,
pleasures and pursuits to enrich it,
and families and friends with which to share it.

Receive our praise,
and accept our worship.
We thank you for one another here,
for the faith that we share,
the fellowship we enjoy,
the Lord we serve,
and the call that unites us.
Receive our praise,
and accept our worship.
Great and wonderful God,
you have blessed us in more ways
than we can ever begin to number,
your goodness greater than we can ever hope to measure,
your love beyond anything we can even begin to fathom,
and yet we know you as a living reality in our hearts,
as the one who gives shape and purpose to all of life.
So we come to you with grateful hearts in joyful homage,
seeking, as best we can, to make our response.
Receive our praise,
and accept our worship.
Through Jesus Christ our Lord. *Nick Fawcett*

222 Sovereign God,
we come into your presence reminded of your greatness,
your holiness,
your beauty
and your love;
conscious that we come into the presence
of one vastly greater than ourselves;
the creator of life and sustainer of the universe,
of everything that is and has been and shall be.
For all that we have received,
we thank you.
You are a God of justice and truth, righteousness and purity,
and yet we remember that you are also a God of love –
a God who cares for each one of us,
bringing joy out of sadness,
hope out of despair,
light out of darkness,
wholeness out of imperfection.

Day by day you are with us,
at work in the lives of all.
For all that we have received,
we thank you.
We thank you for the many blessings you pour into our lives,
for the innumerable gifts that enrich them –
the love we share,
the beauty we marvel at,
the health we enjoy,
the interests we pursue –
so much to excite and enthral,
to fascinate and savour;
so much to give thanks for!
For all that we have received,
we thank you.
We thank you that in Christ we are set free
truly to appreciate your world –
that the bondage of sin,
the stranglehold of self
and the grip of death have been broken.
We thank you that you want us to enjoy life at its fullest,
and not just now but for all eternity.
Great is your name and worthy of all honour and glory.
For all that we have received,
we thank you.
To you be praise and thanksgiving,
power and dominion,
now and for ever. *Nick Fawcett*

223 Loving God,
we thank you for this new day and all the opportunities
it brings –
a time to rest and unwind,
to rejoice and celebrate,
to reflect and worship,
to share with family and friends,
to meet with one another and with you.
For this and every moment,
we bring you our grateful praise.

We thank you for having been with us over the days
gone by –
always there by our side
to guide our footsteps,
give light to our path,
and lead us forward.
For this and every moment,
we bring you our grateful praise.
We thank you for the assurance
that you will be with us in the days ahead –
that, whatever they may bring,
whatever challenges we may face, or trials we may endure,
you will be there to see us through,
giving us the strength and the resources we need,
and a joy that cannot be shaken.
For this and every moment,
we bring you our grateful praise.
We thank you that you are God of past, present and future,
the same yesterday, today and tomorrow,
and in that faith we welcome this new day,
receiving it as your gift,
and consecrating it to your service.
For this and every moment,
we bring you our grateful praise.
Through Jesus Christ our Lord. *Nick Fawcett*

224 Loving God,
we have so many things to thank you for,
more than we can ever begin to number,
and there is so much we have not yet even started to explore!
For all the joys that are yet in store,
gratefully, we praise you.
We thank you for the wonder of life –
for the fact that it is able to thrill and move us in
countless ways,
constantly offering fresh experiences,
new joys,
unimagined opportunities.
No matter who we are or what we have done,

there are still untold riches waiting to be tapped –
places to visit, people to meet,
pleasures to taste, possibilities to explore –
far more than we can ever exhaust in this life's fleeting span.
For all the joys that are yet in store,
gratefully, we praise you.
We thank you for the wonder of your love –
for the fact that it too is able to thrill and move us
in innumerable ways,
once more offering fresh experiences,
new joys,
unimagined opportunities.
No matter who we are or what we have done,
there are still untold riches waiting to be tapped –
faith to explore, fellowship to enjoy,
forgiveness to receive, fulfilment to discover –
far more than we can ever ask for or imagine,
and spanning all eternity.
For all the joys that are yet in store,
gratefully, we praise you.
Loving God,
we do not know what lies ahead,
except that there will be a mixture of good and bad,
joys and sorrows.
But what we know for certain is that, in life or in death,
you will be with us,
always waiting to enrich our lives,
always seeking to deepen our happiness,
and ultimately bestowing on us untold blessings.
For all the joys that are yet in store,
gratefully, we praise you.
In the name of Christ our Lord. *Nick Fawcett*

225 Lord of all,
you are a God of power,
mighty and mysterious,
and we thank you for that truth,
for the knowledge that you are sovereign over all.

But we thank you also that you are a God of peace,
a God whom we can meet in stillness and silence,
and who speaks in a voice like a gentle whisper.
Draw near to us in the quietness,
and may we hear your voice.

(Silence)

Teach us to make time and space for you –
the opportunity to pause and ponder,
to take stock of our lives,
to reflect on your goodness,
and to understand what it is that you would say to us.
Draw near to us in the quietness,
and may we hear your voice.

(Silence)

Help us to be aware of your presence here among us,
and, through meeting with you now,
may we live each day,
each moment,
in the knowledge that you are always by our side.
Teach us to share every moment with you,
confident that you are there,
and that you care about our welfare.
Draw near to us in the quietness,
and may we hear your voice.

(Silence)

Teach us to bring our prayers to you,
not just today but every day;
to speak freely, openly and spontaneously
of what is in our hearts,
knowing that you delight to hear us.
And teach us also to listen,
humbly, reverently, attentively, eagerly,
certain that you will respond to our cry,
and that, in your own time, you will give us your answer.
Draw near to us in the quietness,
and may we hear your voice.

(Silence)

Help us to use all times such as this,
so that we may grow closer to you,
and so that prayer may not be some occasional activity,
still less some formal duty,
but a joyful relationship
and a constant experience of your renewing love deep within.
Draw near to us in the quietness,
and may we hear your voice.

(Silence)

Lord of all,
we have come in the quietness.
Go with us now into the turmoil of life,
with all its noise and confusion,
all its demands and responsibilities,
and may your peace rest with us there,
this day and for evermore.
Through Jesus Christ our Lord. *Nick Fawcett*

226 God of grace, teach us to hold aloft the torch of faith, bearing it with pride and fervour. Help us to do our bit, through word and deed faithfully handing it on, so that others might receive and pass it on in turn: a flame of love, symbol of hope and beacon of truth – light for all the world. *Nick Fawcett*

227 Living God, you have given us good news, the message of your love in Christ. Wherever the opportunity arises, teach us to share it. *Nick Fawcett*

228 God of all, thank you that, in your eyes, no one is first or second class; that there is no elite few elevated at the expense of others. Thank you that, whatever their station in life, you treat everyone equally, reaching out in love and inviting a response. Teach us not to think too much of ourselves, but also not to think too little, remembering instead that you value us, and all. *Nick Fawcett*

229 Lord Jesus Christ, thank you for seeing beneath the surface to who we really are; for focusing not on the ugliness that disfigures our lives but recognising instead someone of infinite worth, precious enough for you to die for. Teach us, in turn, to see the good in others – the best rather than the worst – looking beyond appearances to the beauty hidden in all. *Nick Fawcett*

230 Gracious God, teach us to stand tall, in full assurance of our worth. However ordinary we may be or average feel, help us to respect ourselves, recognising that you value us as you value all. *Nick Fawcett*

231 Lord God, there are so many wonderful things
in your creation that we take for granted.
Open our eyes to see it all
as an expression of your love for us,
and help us to live thankfully. *Susan Sayers*

232 Lord, we thank you
for the extraordinary generosity of your love,
which takes us by surprise and refreshes us,
and which always appears
where we least think to look for it. *Susan Sayers*

233 Lord, we thank you
that we can trust you completely
and you never let us down! *Susan Sayers*

234 We give you thanks, Lord God,
that you always provide the grace we need
to accomplish what you ask of us. *Susan Sayers*

235 Thank you, loving God,
for the world we live in,
for the colours and shapes,
the sounds and textures in it.
Thank you for giving us minds and emotions
and help us to reverence the whole of creation. *Susan Sayers*

236 Lord God, we pray for more thankful hearts
to bless you, because the gifts we receive from you
are so much more than we deserve. *Susan Sayers*

237 As you learn more about the
universe, thank God for it all. *Susan Sayers*

238 As you grow stronger
and can do more things,
thank God for
making it possible. *Susan Sayers*

239 Thank you, loving God,
for showing us the way to love
and giving us opportunities to give,
to take second place,
to accept people as they are,
to forgive them when they annoy us,
and look for their needs before our own. *Susan Sayers*

240 We bless you for the sun:
its source of fire,
its beams of light,
its rays of warmth.
We bless you for water:
when it is ice,
when it is steam,
when it is flowing free.
We bless you for a human being:
the thinking being,
the doing being,
the feeling being.
We bless you for the Triune God:
the Triune who creates,
the Triune who takes flesh,
the Triune who empowers. *Ray Simpson*

241 Power of powers
we worship you.
Light of lights
we worship you.
Life of lives
we worship you.
Source of life
we turn to you.
Saviour of life
we turn to you.
Sustainer of life
we turn to you.
Love before time
we adore you.
Love in darkest time
we adore you.
Love in this time
we adore you

Ray Simpson

242 Eternal Love Maker,
eternal Love Mate,
eternal Love Messenger,
Three of Limitless Love,
we can glimpse your reflection in
a tender kiss,
a warm embrace,
sporting comradeship,
an adult affirming a child,
a meal shared,
two people listening to each other,
a group making music,
hospitality,
young people serving the old,
black and white people celebrating.
Three of Limitless Love,
may we reflect more of you
in whose likeness we are made.

Ray Simpson

243 As nature laughs in spring,
restore laughter to our lives.
When we become complaining and sour-faced,
put something funny into our minds.
Help us not to take ourselves too seriously
and to enjoy the world with you. *Ray Simpson*

244 Make us eager to align our wills with yours.
Give us joy in our hearts, keep us serving.
May we grow in intimacy with you
until every one of our acts
is a glad response to your promptings. *Ray Simpson*

245 Source of Creativity,
teach us
to dance with the playful clouds
and to laugh with the glinting sun.
Teach us
to flow like the sparkling streams
and to soar like the high-winged birds.
Teach us
to dream of rainbow and mountain
and to attempt what we see.
Teach us
to restock memory's treasure-house
and to give it all away. *Ray Simpson*

246 God make us fit for purpose,
alive in heart and limb.
God stretch our creaking bodies
till they tingle and feel trim.
Put fibre in our being,
take flabbiness away.
Strengthen what is weak,
keep binge and bulge at bay.
May each body be a temple
of your Spirit who is true;
a picture frame on Earth
of eternity on view. *Ray Simpson*

247 Remove the clutter from our lives, Lord,
and give us the grace of Blessed Simplicity.
Remove the divided affections from our lives, Lord,
and give us the grace of undivided love for all.
Remove the dominating spirit from our lives, Lord,
and give us the grace of seeking the good in the other.

Ray Simpson

248 Divine Saviour, your birth in the stable at Bethlehem
reveals the simplicity of the Father's love.
Help us, like you, to fling away burdensome accessories
and live in simplicity and joy. *Ray Simpson*

249 Holy God,
help us to live at the still centre
of the world's whirring wheels,
where everything is led by you,
where all is one and we are at peace. *Ray Simpson*

250 Lord of Earth and heaven,
the food we eat is earth, water and air,
coming to us through pleasing plants or creatures.
When we eat, help us to keep these in mind
and to keep it simple. *Ray Simpson*

251 Restore to us, O God,
your rhythms that we have lost:
the rhythm of rising and sleeping;
the rhythm of rest and work;
the rhythm of breathing and walking;
the rhythm of quiet and speech;
the rhythm of loving and losing;
the rhythm of light and dark. *Ray Simpson*

252 Blessing of discovery be yours,
and blessing of rest.
Blessing of scenery be yours,
and blessing of saints.

Blessing of meeting be yours,
and blessing of solitude.
Blessing of friendship be yours,
and blessing of thought. *Ray Simpson*

253 Babe of Heaven,
strengthen us on our pilgrimage.
Your birth shows us
the simplicity of the Father's love,
the wonder of being human.
Help us to live fully human lives for you.
We quieten our souls under the stillness of sky
and we nestle with you in the Father's lap. *Ray Simpson*

254 In the silence, we become aware of you, O God.
In the silence, we adore you.
In the silence, our sins stand out and are washed away.
In the silence, our problems fall into their rightful place.
In the silence, we become grateful people.
In the silence, O Lord, we become one with you
and we catch the whispers of your heart. *Ray Simpson*

255 The welcome of the Father's arms be ours.
The welcome of the Saviour's heart be ours.
The welcome of the Spirit's call be with us.
Deep peace of this earth to us.
Deep peace of this sky to us.
Deep peace of this place to us.
The kindly eye of the Three be upon us,
to aid us and guard us,
to cherish and enrich us.
May God take us in the clasp
of his own two hands. *Ray Simpson*

256 Beauty of friendship, grow between us,
friendship without guile,
friendship without malice,
friendship without striving.

Goodness of friendship, grow between us,
friendship with insight,
friendship with faithfulness,
friendship with the light touch. *Ray Simpson*

257 Be in the eye of each friend on our journey,
to bless and to teach each one.
The eye of the Father be upon us.
The eye of the Son be upon us.
The eye of the Spirit be upon us.
The eye of the Friendly Three
be upon us for ever. *Ray Simpson*

258 Eternal Friend,
we thank you for the countless people who,
through the human gift of friendship,
have turned into your friends.
Renew in us the gift of friendship,
and draw many folk in to the circle of your love.
Ray Simpson

259 For the glory of creation
streaming from your heart,
we praise you.
For the air of the eternal
seeping through the physical,
we praise you.
For the everlasting glory
dipping into time,
we praise you.
For the wonder of your presence
beckoning from each leaf,
we praise you.
For setting us,
like the stars in their courses,
within the orbit of your love,
we praise you. *Ray Simpson*

260 Lord of the Dance, grant me joy in all things:
in the towel that rubs my body,
the steam that heats my coffee,
the street that greets my feet
and the wonder of a life.
Echoes words on a Seattle plaque Ray Simpson

261 We give you thanks for great moments of grace
in the evolution of the cosmos.
For the death of a star
which brought to birth planet Earth.
For the emergence of life forms.
For the emergence of minerals,
vegetables and animals.
For the cooperation,
and not just the competition,
between all that lives.
We give thanks for the moments of grace
in the life of a person;
the power of attraction and the wonder of a birth.
For the human person,
endowed with conscience, awe and intelligence,
a co-creator with you. *Ray Simpson*

262 Unto you, O Lord, be praise for
every flower that ever grew,
every bird that ever flew,
every wind that ever blew.
Unto you, O Lord, be praise for
every flake of virgin snow,
every place where humans go,
every joy and every woe.
Unto you, O Lord, be praise for
every life that shall be born,
every heart that shall be torn,
every day and every dawn.
Echoes an early Irish prayer *Ray Simpson*

263 Maker of all creatures, we honour you.
Friend of all creatures, we honour you.
Force of all creatures, we honour you. *Ray Simpson*

264 I thank you for the wind
that clears the fogs of life,
for chimneys that allow air and warmth
to move through our lives,
for the texture of the bricks,
tiles and wood that breathe.
I thank you for housetops and street lights
and for the sound of traffic moving.
I thank you for Internet, TV and satellite dishes
that open the world up
to people in their little dwellings.
So much energy, so much enterprise –
the friendly smiles of Sister Earth. *Ray Simpson*

265 Thank you,
Creator of the world,
for the music and medicine of flowers,
which give us a scent of heaven upon Earth;
and for their vases which enable them to give their best.
May those who look at them see your glory. *Ray Simpson*

266 For the beauty and bounty of the world,
its seasons and its gifts;
for the wonder of life
and the Earth on which we live:
we offer you our heartfelt praise. *Ray Simpson*

267 Thank you for
the taste of good food,
the crying of the wind
and the pulsing of our bodies.
Thank you for the cartwheels of the heart
the playing of a child
and the diving of a fish. *Ray Simpson*

268 God bless the earth that is beneath us,
the sky that is above us,
the life that lies before us,
your image deep within us.

Echoes a traditional Scottish blessing *Ray Simpson*

269 May the blessing of the rain be on us,
the sweet soft rain.
May it fall upon our spirits
so that all the little flowers may spring up
and shed their sweetness on the air.
May the blessing of the great rains be upon us,
that they beat upon our spirits
and wash them fair and clean,
and leave there many a shining pool
where the blue of heaven shines,
and sometimes a star.

Echoes a traditional Irish blessing *Ray Simpson*

270 A thousand thanks to you,
O King of the universe.
A thousand thanks to you,
O Lord of grace,
for what you have given us since our birth,
and for what you will give us
until the day of our death. *Ray Simpson*

271 Thanks be to you, O God,
praise be to you, O God,
reverence be to you, O God,
for all you have given us.
As you have given physical life
to earn us our worldly food,
so grant us eternal life
to show forth your glory. *Ray Simpson*

272 You made the Earth, and through the long ages
planted it with every kind of plant.
You made animals to crawl and to run upon it,
birds to fly over it and fish to swim around it.

When all was prepared,
you formed humankind from the soil.
You breathed your life into them.
May we never forget that we are mortal creatures;
from earth we come, to earth we go.
We did not make ourselves.
We and the Earth need to be redeemed
through the Saviour who restores unity
between Earth and heaven.
Saviour, bless and redeem us. *Ray Simpson*

273 May we love you in your Earth
and in every grain of sand.
May we love you in your skies
and in every ray of light.
May we love you in the animals
and in everything that breathes.
May we love you in your plants
and in every leaf that greens.
May we love you in your creation
and in the symphony of the whole.
May we love you for yourself
and in your infinite Being. *Ray Simpson*

274 Peace to the land and all that grows on it.
Peace to the sea and all that swims in it.
Peace to the air and all that flies through it.
Peace with our God who calls us to serve. *Ray Simpson*

275 Peace between believers;
peace between neighbours;
peace between lovers;
in love of the King of Life.
Peace between person and person;
peace between wife and husband;
peace between parents and children;
the peace of Christ above all peace. *Ray Simpson*

276 Peace between parties,
peace between neighbours,
peace between lovers,
in love of the King of Life.
Peace between peoples,
peace between traditions,
peace between generations,
in love of the Lord of all. *Ray Simpson*

277 Deep peace of the quiet earth,
deep peace of the still waters,
deep peace of the setting sun,
deep peace of the forgiving heart,
deep peace of the true call,
deep peace of the Son of Peace
be ours, today, for ever. *Ray Simpson*

278 Deep peace of the warming sun to you.
Deep peace of the pure white moon to you.
Deep peace of the shining stars to you.
Deep peace of the cleansing winds to you.
Deep peace of the quiet earth to you.
Deep peace of the knowing stones to you.
Deep peace of the forgiving heart to you.
Deep peace of the Son of Peace to you.
Deep peace.

Echoes a prayer of Fiona McLeod *Ray Simpson*

279 Deep peace of the green-blue sea,
deep peace of the rising sun,
deep peace of the shoreside Christ,
deep peace of the Risen One
be ours today. *Ray Simpson*

280 Deep peace of the setting sun,
deep peace of the forgiving heart,
deep peace of the lakeside Christ
be ours, today, for ever. *Ray Simpson*

281 Deep peace of the Spirit to you.
Peace of the air flowing out to you.
Peace of the Son growing strong in you. *Ray Simpson*

282 The joy of memory be yours today,
the joy of growth along the way.
Forgiveness be yours for failings past,
fruit be yours that will always last.
May that day when you embarked
be also a day that in heaven is marked.
The joy of that day be in your face,
the joy that made you grow in grace. *Ray Simpson*

283 On this, your anniversary,
God give you the best of memories,
Christ give you pardon for failings,
Spirit give you the fruits of friendship. *Ray Simpson*

284 Joy of birth be yours today.
Joy of memory be yours today.
Joy of life be yours today.
Joy of goodness be yours today.
Joy of creation be yours today.
Joy of friendship be yours today.
Joy of giving be yours today.
Joy of maturing be yours today.
Joy of being known be yours today.
Joy of self-knowing be yours today.
Joy of Shepherd Father be yours today.
Joy of Mary's Son be yours today.
Joy of Friendly Spirit be yours today.
Joy of eternal life be yours today
and for ever. *Ray Simpson*

285 Lead me, Lord, into a place of prayer,
to live simply, silently and alone with you,
so that I may die to myself quicker
and Christ may grow in me faster;
so that you may give more of him
to the world that hungers for him.
Echoes words of Catherine Doherty *Ray Simpson*

286 You, Lord, burn in this place.
Your presence fills it.
Strip from me all that is not of you.
Call me to whatever you will.
Lead me wherever you will. *Ray Simpson*

287 God, make my heart a little cell.
Keep harm without, keep peace within.
God, make my heart an altar
where I may gaze into your face.
God, make my heart your home
where I am content to be with you *Ray Simpson*

288 The sun rides high and long,
a sign of blessing from our God.
Everything that breathes cries 'Yes!'
At day's fading we cry 'Yes' to Christ,
the eternal Sun. *Ray Simpson*

289 A blessing on the season of growth,
on all that is done and felt,
the blessing of the fertile Creator,
the blessing of the virile Son,
the blessing of the Spirit, the sustaining One. *Ray Simpson*

290 We give thanks for the growth of sunlit days.
We offer you the first of our crops
and the best of our lives –
all that we have, all that we are –
for all things come from you,
and of your own do we give you. *Ray Simpson*

291 As we enter this season of creativity,
may we think your thoughts after you.
As we explore new realms of life,
may we sense your Spirit after you.
As we enter our beds of hope,
may we dream your dreams after you. *Ray Simpson*

292 God of the summer,
may this be for us
a season of growth and friendship,
a season of activity and celebration.
May vigour and chivalrous love
flow strongly in our veins.
May heroes and holy ones
urge us on to give our all.

Ray Simpson

293 Life of Jesus, Sun of suns,
filling every part of us,
life be in our speech,
sense in what we say.
Love be in our deeds
till you come back again.
Love of Jesus, Sun of suns,
filling every heart for us,
love be in our deeds,
thought be in our words.
Care be in our mien
till you come back again.

Ray Simpson

294 To the Sun of suns, come,
singing Jesus is Lord.
Earth, come to the sun's king,
singing Jesus is Lord.
Sky, come to the sun's king,
singing Jesus is Lord.
Spirits, come to the sun's king,
singing Jesus is Lord.
Birther, Saviour,
lighting Spirit, you are the Lord.

Ray Simpson

295 Sun shines,
sap rises,
buds burst,
lambs frolic,
birds sing,
people play.
Glory to God
who sustains and nurtures us all.

Ray Simpson

296 God of goodness,
the wonders of your creation,
the splendour of the heavens,
the order and richness of nature
speak to us of your glory.
The coming of your Son,
the presence of your Spirit,
the fellowship of your Church
show us the marvel of your love.
The patterns of the year,
the beauty of the Earth,
the ripening gifts of harvest
call us to worship and adore you.
Hear our heartfelt 'Amen'. *Ray Simpson*

297 Thank you for harvest's boundless store,
and the fruits of the Earth
which sustain and gladden us.
Thank you for those who work the land
or are part of the food chain that reaches to our door.
Thank you for comforts of life
and the power to help others.
Thank you for your creation
and the One you sent to restore us
when we fell away from your plan. *Ray Simpson*

298 May this season of mellow fruitfulness
enrich and bless us.
May we harvest relationships of trust,
forgiveness and generosity.
And, until we meet again,
may we be kept in the hollow of God's hand. *Ray Simpson*

299 Thank you for a roof over our head,
for firm earth under our tread,
for supplies to fill our hunger,
for friends to assuage our anger. *Ray Simpson*

300 As the trees are stripped of foliage,
may we be stripped of clutter.
As the leaves fall to the ground,
may we fall into your lap.
As the crops ready for harvest are gathered,
may the wisdom of our days be garnered. *Ray Simpson*